ECLIPSES

Julie Kentner

childsworld.com

The Child's World
childsworld.com

Published by The Child's World®
800-599-READ • www.childsworld.com

Photography Credits
Photographs ©: Aubrey Gemignani/NASA, cover, 1, 17; Gwen Pitman/NASA, 2–3; Joel Kowsky/NASA, 5; Jordan Salkin/NASA, 6; Albert Stephen Julius/Shutterstock Images, 9, 11; Michael DeMocker/NASA, 12; Bill Ingalls/NASA, 14; Norah Moran/NASA, 15; Patrick T. Fallon/AFP/Getty Images, 18; Jon Nalick/Shutterstock Images, 19; Bill Hrybyk/NASA, 20

ISBN Information
9781503894402 (Reinforced Library Binding)
9781503895140 (Portable Document Format)
9781503895966 (Online Multi-user eBook)
9781503896789 (Electronic Publication)

LCCN 2024941362

Printed in the United States of America

Bringing the World to Young Readers 1968

ABOUT THE AUTHOR

Julie Kentner is a writer who loves to read. She studied archaeology in university. She lives in Winnipeg, Manitoba, Canada, with her husband and their cats.

CONTENTS

CHAPTER ONE

A TOTAL ECLIPSE!

On April 8, 2024, more than 50,000 people gathered at the Indianapolis Motor Speedway. This famous racetrack is in Indianapolis, Indiana. Many of the people had cameras. They were wearing special glasses to protect their eyes.

The sky began to get darker. People could see the Moon passing in front of the Sun. Soon, they could see only half of the Sun. The sky kept getting darker. Finally, the Moon blocked the whole Sun. The eclipse was in totality. It was afternoon. But the sky looked like a sunset in every direction. The air grew cooler.

A glowing haze appeared around the Moon. People were cheering. It stayed dark for almost 4 minutes. Then the Moon kept moving, and more of the Sun began to reappear. Everyone was excited. They had just seen a total solar eclipse!

People who watched the eclipse at the Indianapolis Motor Speedway got to see race cars drive before the main event.

The Sun is 400 times wider than the Moon. But the Sun is 400 times farther away. Because of this, the Sun and the Moon appear to be the same size during a solar eclipse.

Eclipses happen when the Sun, the Moon, and the Earth line up in space. There are two types of eclipses. These are solar and lunar eclipses. In a solar eclipse, the Moon passes between the Earth and the Sun. This makes it look as if the Moon is covering up the Sun. The Moon's shadow hits the Earth. As the Earth **rotates**, the shadow moves across it. People near the shadow's edges see a partial eclipse.

In a partial eclipse, only part of the Sun is covered. For people in the shadow's center, the Moon fully blocks the Sun. The time when the Moon and Sun completely overlap is called totality. Solar eclipse totality is usually under 10 minutes. After that time, the Moon moves past the Sun. The light returns again, and the eclipse is over.

The second type of eclipse is a lunar eclipse. In a lunar eclipse, the Earth is between the Sun and the Moon. The Earth casts a shadow on the Moon. Sometimes, the Earth blocks only part of the Sun's light. Other times, all the light from the Sun is blocked by the Earth. Lunar eclipse totality can last from 30 minutes to more than an hour. During a lunar eclipse, the moon can appear dark and even red.

Eclipses can be seen all over the world at certain times. Scientists can **predict** when an eclipse will appear. The science behind how eclipses form determines when they will be visible.

THE POWER OF ECLIPSES

Eclipses have affected history. Thousands of years ago, two groups were fighting in Greece. Then, a solar eclipse happened. The two sides became very afraid. No one understood what was happening! Everyone stopped fighting and reached a peace agreement.

CHAPTER TWO

HOW ECLIPSES HAPPEN

The Earth travels in an **orbit** around the Sun. The Moon travels in an orbit around the Earth. As these objects orbit, the distances between the Sun, the Moon, and the Earth change. The distances between these space objects affects what kind of eclipse can happen.

The Sun, Moon, and Earth line up every month. But there is not a solar eclipse every month. This is because the Moon's orbit is **tilted**. This changes how its shadow falls on the Earth. Sometimes the Moon is higher than the Earth. Sometimes it is lower. Other times, it lines up directly between the Earth and the Sun. This is when a solar eclipse happens.

For a solar eclipse to happen, the Moon must line up directly between the Sun and the Earth. But because its orbit is tilted, the Moon is often too high or too low to cause an eclipse.

Solar eclipses can be total, annular, or partial. Lunar eclipses can be total or partial. In a total solar eclipse, the Moon looks as if it is the same size as the Sun. When the Moon comes between the Sun and the Earth, it completely blocks the Sun.

During an annular eclipse, the Moon is as far from the Earth as it can be. The Sun is as close to the Earth as it can be. This makes the Moon look smaller in the sky. When the Moon comes between the Sun and the Earth, it does not completely cover the Sun. A ring of light is still visible around the Moon's edges. Because of this, annular eclipses are sometimes called "ring of fire" eclipses.

During an eclipse, the Earth or the Moon casts a shadow. The darkest part of this shadow is called the umbra. Around the umbra is a lighter shadow. This area is called the penumbra. People in a place where the umbral shadow falls will see a total eclipse. People in a place where the penumbral shadow falls will see a partial eclipse.

THE GEOMETRY OF AN ECLIPSE

SOLAR ECLIPSE

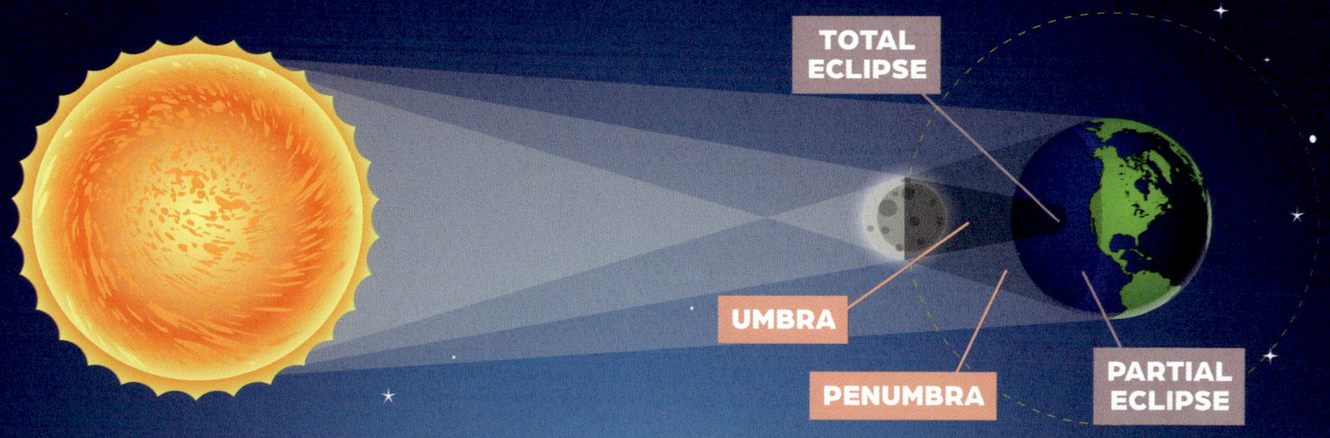

The Moon passes directly between the Sun and the Earth. The Moon's shadow hits the Earth. The darkest area of the shadow is the umbra. This is the area experiencing a total eclipse. The lighter area of the shadow is the penumbra. This is the area experiencing a partial eclipse.

LUNAR ECLIPSE

The Moon revolves around the Earth. It passes through the Earth's shadow. The darkest area of the shadow is the umbra. The lighter area of the shadow is the penumbra

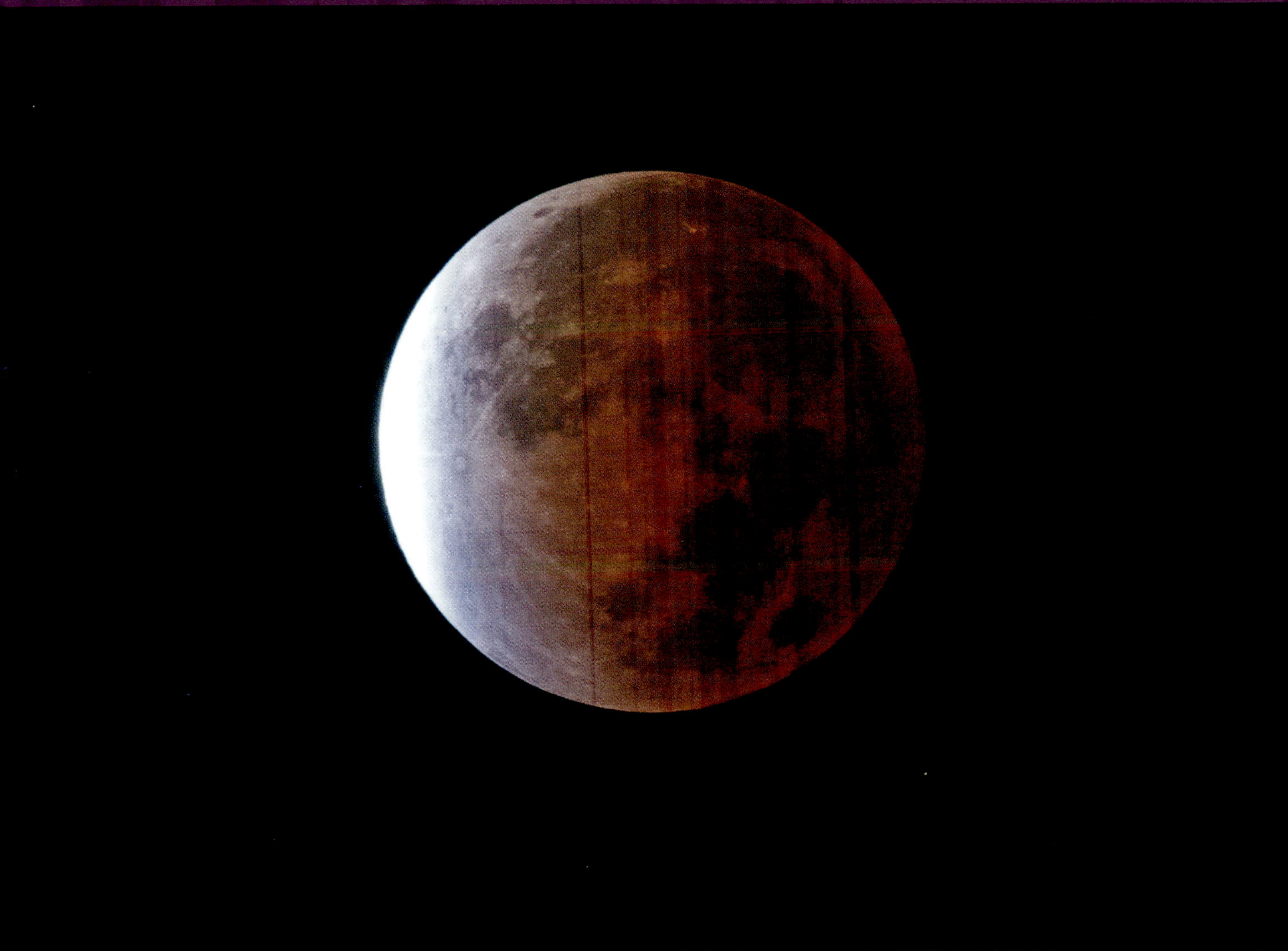

There are no annular lunar eclipses because the Earth is much larger than the Moon. Its shadow will never be small enough to leave a ring.

During a total lunar eclipse, the Moon often looks red. This is because of Earth's **atmosphere**. The light that comes from the Sun looks white. But it is actually made up of the colors of the rainbow. Each color of light travels at a different speed. The gases in Earth's atmosphere scatter the light from the Sun. Blue light scatters more than the other colors. This is why the sky is usually blue. At sunset, the Sun's light has to travel through more layers of the atmosphere. The blue light is scattered away. But red, orange, and yellow light get through. This is why the sky turns different colors at sunset. A similar effect happens during a lunar eclipse. The only light from the Sun that reaches the Moon passes through Earth's atmosphere. The atmosphere scatters the blue light away. The red light is left behind.

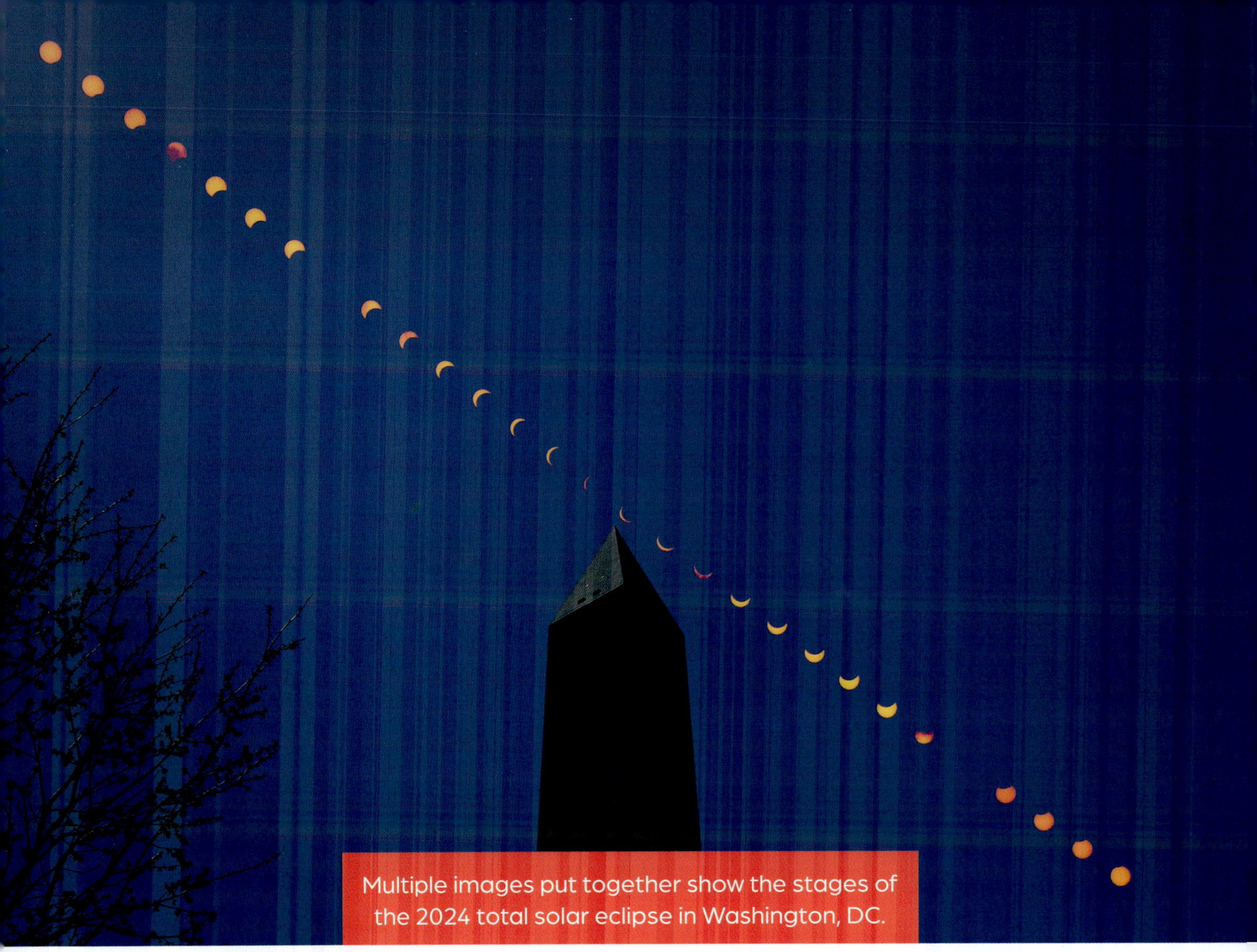

Multiple images put together show the stages of the 2024 total solar eclipse in Washington, DC.

Two to five solar eclipses happen every year. A total solar eclipse happens around every 18 months. But people have to be in the right place at the right time to see a solar eclipse. The penumbral shadow is small, and the umbral shadow is even smaller. Because of this, solar eclipses are only visible in a small area. A total solar eclipse can be seen from any one place every 400 years.

Lunar eclipses are much easier to see. Earth's penumbral shadow covers the whole Moon. The eclipse will be visible from anywhere it is nighttime. Lunar eclipses happen less often than solar eclipses. But because they are easier to see, they seem more common.

For thousands of years, people have told stories to explain why eclipses happen. Some people thought gods made an eclipse happen. Others said animals were eating the Moon.

CHAPTER THREE

WHERE TO SEE AN ECLIPSE

Eclipses do not happen every day. But scientists can predict when an eclipse will take place. They learn where it will appear. People can travel to see eclipses based on these predictions.

People throughout history have predicted eclipses. Thousands of years ago, people made predictions by keeping track of when the Sun and Moon crossed. These predictions gave only a general idea of when an eclipse would take place. Over time, people realized eclipses happen according to a **cycle**. Solar and lunar eclipses would take place approximately 9 years apart. Similar solar eclipses happened every 18 years. This is because the Sun and the Moon returned to the same place in the sky every 18 years. This cycle is called the Saros cycle. Scientists eventually learned that a Saros cycle is 18 years, 11 days, and 8 hours.

Multiple images put together show the stages of the 2017 eclipse in Madras, Oregon.

Today, computers with special software can **calculate** exactly when and where an eclipse will happen.

A total solar eclipse crossed the United States on August 21, 2017. The path of totality stretched from Oregon to North Carolina. Approximately 12 million people lived in the totality zone. More than 200 million adults watched the eclipse in person or online. It lasted for nearly 3 minutes.

Some parts of the United States saw two solar eclipses in 6 months. On October 14, 2023, an annular eclipse crossed parts of North, Central, and South America. Millions of people lived in the path of the eclipse. Then on April 8, 2024, a total solar eclipse passed over parts of Mexico, the United States, and eastern Canada. Thousands of people traveled to see it. The Moon blocked the Sun for nearly 4 minutes.

In Albuquerque, New Mexico, the 2023 eclipse lined up with the International Balloon Fiesta. This is the largest hot-air balloon festival in the world. It was too windy to fly. But pilots lit their burners to celebrate the eclipse.

People can see multiple eclipse shadows when using a colander as a pinhole projector.

Lunar eclipses do not require special equipment for viewing. But solar eclipses can be dangerous. Looking directly at the Sun may damage a person's vision. The safest way to view a solar eclipse is with a pinhole projector. To use a pinhole projector, people stand with their back to the Sun. They let sunlight shine through a small hole. This can be a hole punched in a piece of paper or cardboard. People can also use their hands or a colander as a pinhole projector. They can see the shadow of the eclipse on the ground.

Eclipse glasses allow people to safely look at the Sun during a solar eclipse.

Some people want to see more than the shadow. To look directly at the Sun, people need special eye protection. Sunglasses are not enough. Viewers must wear special eclipse glasses. These are thousands of times darker than sunglasses. Some companies sell fake eclipse glasses. These are not dark enough to protect people's eyes. People should make sure their glasses are real before using them. While wearing real eclipse glasses, a person inside would not be able to see anything except bright lights. A person outside should not see anything but the Sun or its reflection.

Wearing eclipse glasses is not enough to use cameras, binoculars, or telescopes safely. Each of these needs a special **filter**. These solar filters protect the equipment and prevent eye damage.

An eclipse is more than an exciting show. Total solar eclipses allow scientists to study part of the Sun's atmosphere, called the corona. Scientists learn how heat and energy move from the Sun into space. They also study spots on the Sun during eclipses. During a solar eclipse, radio waves have clearer signals. Scientists use radio waves to measure the size of the spots. This helps scientists understand the weather in space. Scientists have also used eclipses to help measure the exact size and the shape of the Sun. Whether they are simply a cool **phenomenon** or a chance for research, eclipses have something to offer everyone.

ECLIPSES FOR SCIENCE

More than 2,000 years ago, Ancient Greeks studied the Earth's shadow on the Moon during a lunar eclipse. They learned that the Earth was round. They also calculated the size of the Moon and how far it was from the Earth.

GLOSSARY

atmosphere (AT-muss-feer) An atmosphere is the layer of gases that surrounds a planet. Blue light gets scattered by Earth's atmosphere, making the sky blue.

calculate (KAL-kyoo-layt) To calculate is to use math and other information to find an answer. Scientists used eclipses to calculate the size of the Moon.

cycle (SYE-kuhl) A cycle is a series of events that are repeated. Eclipses happen in an 18-year cycle.

filter (FILL-tur) A filter is used to block something. A person needs to use a filter to safely view a solar eclipse through a camera or telescope.

orbit (OR-bit) An orbit is the rounded path that an object takes as it goes around a larger object. The Earth is in orbit around the Sun, and the Moon is in orbit around the Earth.

phenomenon (fuh-NAH-muh-nahn) A phenomenon is an observable event that can be explained by science. An eclipse is a phenomenon caused by the positions of the Sun, Moon, and Earth.

predict (prih-DIKT) To predict something is to try to guess what will happen in the future based on observation or experience. Scientists can predict when eclipses will happen.

rotates (ROH-tayts) When something rotates, it turns in a circle around a point in the center. As the Earth rotates, the Moon's shadow moves across it.

tilted (TILL-ted) When something is tilted, it leans to one side. The Moon's orbit is tilted, which is why solar eclipses do not happen every month.

FAST FACTS

- In a solar eclipse, the Moon passes between the Earth and the Sun. The Moon blocks the Sun's light, casting a shadow on Earth.
- In a lunar eclipse, the Earth goes between the Sun and the Moon. The Earth casts a shadow on the Moon.
- Solar eclipses can be total, annular, or partial. In a total eclipse, the Moon completely covers the Sun. In an annular eclipse, a small ring of light is visible around the Moon. In a partial eclipse, only part of the Sun is covered.
- Lunar eclipses can be total or partial.
- Scientists can predict when eclipses will happen.
- Scientists study eclipses to learn more about the Sun, the Earth, and space.

ONE STRIDE FURTHER

- Would you prefer to see a solar eclipse or a lunar eclipse? Why?
- If you could travel anywhere in the world to see an eclipse, where would you go? Why?
- Draw a picture of a solar eclipse and what it would look like if you saw it from your home.
- What would you take with you to view an eclipse? Why?

FIND OUT MORE

IN THE LIBRARY

Allen, Stacy. *Rainbows and Halos*. Parker, CO: The Child's World, 2025.

Betts, Bruce. *Casting Shadows: Solar and Lunar Eclipses with The Planetary Society*. Minneapolis, MN: Lerner, 2024.

Rau, Dana Meachen. *What Is a Solar Eclipse?* New York, NY: Penguin Workshop, 2024.

ON THE WEB

Visit our website for links about eclipses:

childsworld.com/links

Note to Parents, Caregivers, Teachers, and Librarians: We routinely verify our web links to make sure they are safe and active sites. So encourage your readers to check them out!

INDEX